Poems of Wartime Years

With thanks to my editors, publisher and friends
for their support and encouragement.

Poems of Wartime Years

by

W N Taylor

Augur Press

POEMS OF WARTIME YEARS
Copyright © W N Taylor

The moral right of the author has been asserted

British Library Cataloguing in Publication Data.
A catalogue record for this book is available
from the British Library.

ISBN 978-0-9549551-6-8

First published in 2007 by
Augur Press
Delf House
52, Penicuik Road
Roslin
Midlothian EH25 9LH
United Kingdom

Printed by Lightning Source

Preface

My experience of World War 2 was in the Far East – South East Asia Command (SEAC), but these are not 'war poems' in the ordinary sense. They are thoughts and memories of the periphery rather than the centre of action, and reflections afterwards in subsequent years, some pertaining to other wars, bearing the stamp of futility, cynicism, sadness and a flicker of hope.

I was a medical student when the war began in 1939, larking about with my friends (see 'A Cycle of Sonnets'), but knowing that when we qualified we would be called up. After serving with an infantry battalion in coastal defence on the Isle of Wight, I was posted to a West African division and accompanied them into the jungles of Burma. This involved a fight against disease as well as against the Japanese. When this was over, I sailed off with my African soldiers and returned them to their homes in the Gold Coast, now called Ghana. Before demobilisation I served for a short time in a prisoner-of-war camp in Scotland, attending to German prisoners.

It was disconcerting to be back in civilian life. Peace was full of unease, and hardly seemed peaceful. The effect of the war on social life, and upon my reaction to it, was disturbing. Our culture had changed, and I felt that this was not for the better. I was uneasy; and thinking moreover of the international unrest and subsequent wars, I wondered what it was all leading to. I still wonder.

So the war years I have in mind comprise not only those of World War 2, but the many years that have been plagued by wars that have affected us all in one way or another, in our present lives or in our history. However I have tried to avoid making statements purporting to apply to people in general, and have concerned myself with expressing my own reactions. Perhaps these might resonate with what others have been feeling.

CONTENTS

New Forest.. 1

The Lost Seeker 4

Can we limn Life in Beauty?................................... 6

The Dying Phase – 1 7

The Dying Phase – 2 10

Algiers Harbour 12

Arabian Night 13

Troop-ship Idleness 15

Scottish Sailor... 17

Moved by the Glimpse of a Girl 18

Railway Station, Ootacamund 20

A Street Child, India... 22

Sonnet: Jupiter Symphony.................................... 24

Arakan 25

Prayer.. 27

A Shot-up Outpost 28

V Day.. 29

A Lullaby for World War 2 30

Remembrance Day 32

Autumn... 34

Korea 36

The Rebels 38

      Pacifist.. 38

      A Dying Partisan 39

Aftermath.. 40

      War and Peace.. 40

      Sonnet, free style 41

Danger Money 42

Winterreise 43

Blank Verse 44

Separation 45
Fragments 46
    Longing 46
    Loss 47
    Winter 48
    Snow Buntings on the Black Hill 49
    Sheep 50
    The Mountain 51
Advice.. 52
Insomnia 53
The Cynic 58
Insanity 59
Early Spring.. 62
Anger 63
Enigma... 64
Thoughts upon a poem by Yeats 65
Corsica.. 66
    Arrival 66
    Forêt de l'Ospedale 67
    The Tower, Porto... 67
    'Civitas Calvi, Semper Fidelis' 68
Japanese Style.. 70
    Haiku (5-7-5).. 70
    Tanka (5-7-5-7-7) 72
    Linked Verse 72
The Post... 73
A Cycle of Sonnets.. 74
    Duplicity (P.D.K) 74
    Rationality (J.P.D) 75
    Inferiority (R.C.M) 76
    Purity (H.J.M.A)... 77
    Frivolity (R.M.P. & Co.) 78
    Thoughtlessness (B.H.) 79

New Forest - 1943

See traveller where the wood-dove flies
Over these deep-green trees!
Here you can walk the winding, careless road
Where the rose flowers.
Here wander, and glance back,
Turn many corners
On the vague, hilly ribbon of spent time with its green borders
Rich with the souls of men
As the uncut fields are rich,
That speak of heart, not brain. And the willow's switch
Bends to the bright waters.
Here you meet timeless life on the tiny road:
– An old man; whose stubbly pipe sends a thin cloud upwards
That writhes in the heavy air, and melting outwards, drifts
Like happiness, one evanescent moment in the mist;
– Or children's laughter, tinkling as the brook does over pebbles,
Far off in the deeps of summer heat where no thought troubles
The eternity of the hours, and the soul is young and ageless;
– Youth, whose full, firm flesh glows like an autumn apple,
Sits at the foot of a vast beech-cathedral's sky-blue dapple
And there dreams,
Finding the heaven of itself beneath these leaves;
Or meeting the sudden scent of snatched love-episodes
Breathed by roses…wondering to discover
Beauty in sadness; to find pain joy's lover.

1

Old, young, mature mankind, one omnipresent mind,
Fix this instant in time's flux
As you stand in the field tracks.
'We cannot die!' they cry, from the wan depths of time.
And their voice is the leafy rustle of the morning wind:
And their voice wells into the expanded Present; lingering,
Mysteriously wise, carried in morning mist, shimmering,

And like mist dies.

Dies?
But here death is synthesised with birth.
The soul of the whole place, this jewel of rich earth,
Is but the drift of an ageless, timeless being
Breathing through trees and fields and human hearts
Lean with desire for life, and gleams for eyes unseeing –
All quickened by the same fire; living endlessly on.

One twist in the continuum, the apocalypse,
Heaving its blind force passes by;
Leaving its wrung hearts, soft weeping behind closed doors,
Quiet empty rooms, and names on a stone column;
Passes: and still the voices speak in the tree wind,
The pipe-smoke curls, and rose scent overpowers.
The sudden burst of laughter from the woods
Is older, infinitely more old, than the bomb bursting:
The superhuman powers wielded by earth thirsting
Desperately for freedom end in the sudden laughter,
And life goes on anew in the same old manner.
The heap of shattered rubble, the explosion of the bomb,
The martyrdom of armies signal doom…
A simple generation dies, accurst.

But life? Life springs in every flower, as spring it must;
And the old man, the children and the youths
Die and are born again. The soft air soothes;
And seed again brings flowers.

The will of God becalms these shadowy bowers.
The old humanity lives on in the auburn heat of autumn,
Lulled in the leafy shade, and grows like trees
By inches through the years. With closed eyes and deaf ears
Vegetates in the fields – Did you not hear it speak?
Meets you on the quiet road – Did you not meet it then?

SEAC

—o—

The Lost Seeker

Multipotent life,
Polyhedral world,
Word-latticed thought that age has brought
Muttering in a maze of many mirrors:
If as my heritage you lead me to burial,
Cold will my spirit be. Not as in infancy
Strangely, tremendously, it ventured forth.
Now through philosophy, previewing burial,
Forgetting birth,
Coldly detached I stand – shuddering ego
Appalled at oblivion, watching the child that was.

Wondering at the child that was.

Child not yet separate from truth;
(I grown so separate)
Child with a hope untried;
(I a lost seeker)
All life's potential – small,
So seemingly casual!

The sluggish doubting boy, the dreaming girl,
Ambivalent adolescence, brave maturity,
Youth's labour, the quiet memories of age,
Are one within this child.
How then am I alone
Groping in this mirrored maze,
From each glass a ghost thrown back, and a hundred horrors?
Only to see sudden splinters of bright crystal pierce
Occasionally the murk of the meandering years,
Straining the ear to hear truth by candlelight
Whisper whimsically, like the wind?

1944 SEAC

—o—

Can we limn Life in Beauty?

Can we limn life in beauty? Seek to bind
With words the fleeting visions of the mind,
Dredging the long, slow river of eternity?
Is Art futility?
Is the dull soul enriched by questing,
Pitched as it is in the flux of change?
Poetry cannot derange
The awful inevitability of time's halter,
Nor music alter
The grim ambuscade of death.
Why then this breath
Moulded in sound, modulated in language?
If no man can gauge
Truth, why this music?

I have no message.
With a frail instrument, why not knowing,
I can but cage a thought
Suddenly caught
Out of the flowing.

1944 SEAC

—o—

The Dying Phase – 1

Les sanglots longs
Des violins
De l'automne
Blessent mon coeur
D'une langueur
Monotone

　　　　　　　　P. Verlaine

He said 'These fields cry hope,
'There is unending life in the merry wheat!'
But the wind that blew from the sinister hills
Flung a dead leaf at my feet.
Yet I could see the promise of the seasons.

'There is no real death', he said,
'Only the changeless tale of life retold!'
But the importunate wind froze numb my autumn brain,
Cynical and cold.
Yet I could see there would be new creation.

So he looked beyond,
Logically, this other that was me;
The essential promise of the dying phase
I saw, and did not see:
Hope springing the shoot, death winnowing the corn…

This seemed the end for me.

So now…
Leave me to negate and to deny the old values
In this, the dry season of death and non-being:
Roses are cold, putrescent, the dying flesh of summer –
I smell their red blood swelling stagnant veins.
The weeds are blue by dim light between cobble-stones
Growing recklessly in deserted paths where the stones are sprung,
Brushing the famished cat that slinks like a shadow at midnight,
By day still clawing their dusty way to the sun.

In my garden there is only stale air and degradation.
The scarlet fungus is the brightest bloom.
Trees exhale the breath of dead millennia,
Like stalactites in caves: apostates, fugitives from faith,
Rejected and alone.
The flower's corolla, pander to its lust,
Is sick with shrivelled purple;
Lusting, it has died. The beasts have fought and killed.

Whence will tomorrow's wind come?
How many leaves condemned?
The old man said 'There's rain in the wind!'
But no rain came.
This is the dying time. There are dead fruits in the garden
For the dark grubs to gnaw,
And sodden fruits of a poor harvest
Rotting in the orchard of the mind…
Rudely grown in a doomed soil
They drop in tortured autumn with the sun
From unremembered trees. So

Now is the year's forgotten time;
Here are the world's forgotten places;
Rank grass decays; no fair things grow.

There was a time to sow.

1944 In hospital
Secunderabad

—o—

These thick and stagnant mists,
Death's foul miasmata, exhaled
From the rotting flesh of the living,
Rotting in tenements and workhouses,
Rotting in basements and attics,
In factories and at street corners,
In pubs and labour exchanges,
This stench of rotting living
Has made an old man of Time,
A ragged, old grey man with death in his heart,
A dreaded cold old man with a lethal scythe,
Feared because half-welcomed,
Because his cut frees from the choking mist;
Because he means End. And he is old,
As one who has lived too long.
Choked in the clammy mist
Youth fights its living death,
Losing its ephemeral beauties one by one,
Until, intolerant of its bond with life,
It gropes in the foul air for the cold old hand.

O that mankind would realise its duty
To nurture life, and beautify its children!
Not weep sad tears over imagined beauties
Set there in folly by its own corruption;
That it would wake to truth, and make
Not dying bodies, putrefied by time,
But living souls, and bodies of aliveness!
So time would be young and lovely: friend, not enemy.

Summer 1951

—o—

Algiers Harbour, 1943

How plain your eyes speak, soldier,
That stare across the sea!
Far into the bright North West –
You would have snow, I see:
So speak those dim nostalgic eyes,
Blind to the glorious southern skies
And the purple southern sea!

You would have snow at Christmas
And frost upon the wall,
And ice-pools in the gutter,
And grey cold over all!
So speak those dim nostalgic eyes,
Blind to the loud, insistent flies
And to the palm-trees tall!

You would have red fires giving
New life to blood and bone,
And loving friends to greet you,
And home when day is done!
So speak those dim nostalgic eyes,
Fixed where the west horizon lies,
So weary and alone.

—o—

Arabian Night

Can you feel that there is glory here
And lack of the unloveliness of home?

This paradisal world would seem enchanted
By virtue, if beauty were godliness, as may be.
Hot lights on the pulse-stirred glass
Writhe into translucent form. O see!
The moon is heralded by a shower of stars
That fall and glitter in the sea!
Soul of romance
You very closely talk to me. I see your jewelled hair
And hear your bangles chink in the night
And feel your breath warm from the rocky hill!

Cradled in soft night-velvet, do you wait for me…
Wait, O wait! My Queen. I have no fear
Of anything unlovely in this place.
Wait for me there, couched on your bed of darkness,
Divine of the divine! That by your Eastern wizardry
My soul will cling, and a body only
Will tomorrow stare at sunset across the turquoise sea,
And watch the islands of our wedding-place dip slowly in the day's
blood,
Wait for me, irresistible, in your home. I come!

Engulfed in the transcendent glories of this place,
I know my paradisal world is thee-enchanted.

1943 Aden

—o—

14

Troop-ship Idleness

And you, woman –
Making your entrance into Life from your cabin in the morning,
You are 'only human'
You admit, when the voice of conscience sounds a warning;
But you admit it in a way
That oozes condescension: Vastly superior; infinitely proud.
No mere human would say
It quite like that, nor pitch the voice quite so loud.
Your clothes are set with the same studied determination as your
features.
You are not shy, are you, when the men look, and are polite?
No. Far from it. (With no rival charm to beat yours
Unfairly), satisfied, proceed to claim your right!
Insecure? Of course not! You are equal
To the worshipped ones at last. No need to pose
As coy, or humble. Go straight ahead! The sequel
May be some major victory – a catch – who knows?
You are quite plain, and you know it well,
But here you wield power over them: intoxicating, new –
How different from the hell
Of home, and the despair with which you grew...
Gone is the envious gloom in which you spent your
Former feminine lusts in naked dreams;
And you are filled with a sense of high adventure
As with a bright desire self-seeking gleams.

Now you are somebody. Practise what you planned.
Conceal self-interest, naturally: you 'Heard the Call' to roam;
Duty bade you 'Serve your Country' in a foreign land…
Where your womanhood, incidentally, will count so much more than at home.
Nevertheless, though most see through you, some of these men might tell
That you are not merely the incarnation of a sex desire,
But behind that lurks a girl who really can sing quite well,
And could have revealed sincerity had one bothered to enquire.

                                        Indian Ocean 1943

                    —o—

Scottish Sailor

My hert's aye homin'
Though the nicht wad tak the will frae me,
Through the storms an' ower the blackenin' sea
I'll still be comin'.

Bide ye awhile;
Keep bricht the lamp, nor let oor fire burn low,
An' ye will licht my way, though I maun go
A thousand mile.

There's nae road back, although I weel may fail
The way I'm farin',
Hopes for the morn abune the screamin' gale
Wi' you I'm sharin'.

Maybe your faithfu' vigil through the nicht
I'll never see;
Maybe you'll never catch wi' strainin' sicht
A blink o' me.

But since ye watch an' wait, I'll struggle yonder;
An' since I struggle, ye will wait an' wonder.
I'll still be comin':
My hert's aye homin'.

13. 6. 52

—o—

17

Moved by the Glimpse of a Girl

I was moved the moment the glimpse passed between us;
But …not surely by this, my pride, so safely frozen
In decent, hard ice-globules of good sense?
No, not by this surely – for look again in your detachment;
Close your eyes, and climb the cold stairs of the brain;
Attain the distant heights of your lone star-lit turret;
Again stand silent in your infinite silences,
And let the view twice-filtered slowly percolate
In fiery droplets to your polished viewing-slide.
Put on your rubber gloves; adjust your gauze mask;
Focus the microscope, with pencil ready to take notes.
Now, studying the phenomenon, you are alive and yet at peace,
The currents of interest darting in their orderly channels.
Knowledge progresses; you are getting somewhere –
Observe the form and habits of the microbe (species humanity).
Infer the motives as conditioned reflexes.
Allow yourself a little latitude (no harm in that); extend
The view, embrace the entire situation. So,
You wonder what is this small central germ,
So sharp and so familiar?
(Is there a mirror in the microscope…?)
You wonder why it laughs? You are distressed?

Oh surely not, my friend!
Not surely by this, my pride, so safely frozen!
So you observe yourself? You are absorbed
In observing yourself. But you are not
In your silent heights, are you? And this is not
Your starlit turret, is it? For the microscope
Is a shaft of light in a midnight café…

You are not seeing yourself, really. The moment has passed.
You are not seeing at all. You are only feeling
Very much alone.

Tomorrow you will view this insignificant episode,
A war-time fantasy, a last-night's picture,
And you'll explain everything very reasonably.
Except that moment.

1945 Poona

—o—

19

Railway Station, Ootacamund

I know that only the frosty chill
And the cold green light are real,
But yet I allow my heart to be paced
By the clang and roar of steam and steel,
And the practical bustling impersonal will
Of clocks and officials and traveller's haste,
And times of departure, and whether or not
The third-class compartment is crowded, when
That corner seat will be filled... You say
'Hurry! You'll get it!' I hesitate. Then
You hand me shyly the sweets that you bought
And the magazines – useful things to build
A barrier to misery...
The whistle blast
Opens the door of my cell. So
Fate has her firing-squad ready now –
Unconcerned engineers, who know
Their weapons. And here it is at last

Attention! The noise reminds me how
A well-drilled squad's feet can crash as one,
With just the faintest rippling, like
The sound of slamming carriage doors.
Numb now. Just one last thing: the stroke
Of death – the end of peace and joy and love.
Poised is the flag… 'Wait! Just one more thing…
Just this…'
But imperceptibly the train has moved.
Waiting for the end, it has already come.

Always it is like this. Faced with an end to be,
Thought abrogating,
We cannot grasp nothingness, but see
Only the waiting.

A Memory, 1945

—o—

21

A Street Child, India

Unsought spark, dropped from the burning flame
Of some god, older than man's centuries,
Feeble into the city's dust she came,
Into a world of darkest mysteries.
A child of innocence, who never knew
For what strange destiny she came to earth,
Nor knew why human passion round her blew
To storm the elements that gave her birth.

Now glows the spark to fire. And ill-designed
To count the dreary days in homes of men,
How often has her burning fancy pined,
Staring through windows, cheek in hand again,
Yearning for other worlds of dreams, unknown,
Of happiness, of freedom and of grace –
When to be chained in bondage, and alone
Is her acceptance by the human race.

Alas for man! For the immortal will
Must surely triumph, nor forget its own.
There is a destiny life must fulfil.
Leave men to tread their sordid world alone.
First then, discover Self, and know the soul
As that of a goddess, pent in human clay,
Acclaim the spirit, and at last be whole,
Casting in peace the earthy dross away.

1944 Calcutta

—o—

Jupiter Symphony

Now that indifferent time reveals
Its slow, impartial justice; and
The slow revolving of the wheels
That rack us, dulls and finally accustoms
Blood and brain and spirit to Fate's hand,
I see the years foreshortened and drawn in,
Perspectives narrowed down to level planes,
The world a painting on a depthless canvas,
Nothing lost and nothing left to win:
But what are losses in the void, and what are gains?
(The fate that spares me takes my friend away).
There are no further worlds to journey in;
And man, unhappy, scarcely knows his pain,
And caring not, he little knows his sin.

1944 Field Hospital, Comilla

—o—

Arakan

How many miles to burning hell?
Anyone can say:
'Through the rustling jungle night,'
But please to show the way...
    'Through dense mixed scrub and elephant grass
    'And everywhere bamboo,
    'The souls of many vanished men
    'Will point the road for you.'
The crickets creak from dusk to dawn
And spectral creatures yell
Where men gone mad from loneliness
Have cut the way to hell.
How many will come back again?
    'Nobody can say;
    'The misty, mazy jungle tracks
    'All lead the other way.'
How many years to nothingness?
    'No matter who can tell;
    'You cannot think, as fever-numbed,
    'You'll find the road to hell.'

Is this the Road to Mandalay?
Romance has gone before,
And killed in ambush by the Nips,
Can comfort me no more...
No light, no path, no human sign,
Nor hope to help me pray:
'Is this the road to bloody hell?
'O please to show the way...
Show me the way through Arakan,
I can no longer see;
The long, long journey back again
Will be too long for me.
Some sluggish river's mangrove swamps
My resting-place shall be.

Burma,1944

—o—

Prayer

Let go, let go,
Take your arms from me, life!
Unclasp your slow
Embrace, and from this strife
Free me. I rip apart
Your grip around my heart.

In agony I tear
The crushing bonds, and cling
A moment in the air,
Trembling, before I fling
Myself into the deep
Dark of my grave, and sleep.

Contain me well
And silence all my tears,
Here where I fell.
Cover my waking fears
With the sleep within thy deeps
No living creature sleeps.

Thoughts of a soldier – World War 2

1951

—o—

A Shot-up Outpost

Life in the jungle screams
With brutal indifference.
Total uncaring teems –
The vermin of violence.

The men are all dead, smeared over the stones.
Soon ants and maggots will polish the white bones.

I noticed outside one man still moved.
He had escaped; but as I watched, he died,
Leaving his corpse lying there
Like a discarded uniform, empty, cast aside.

I felt he mattered to me. But what could I do? He's dead…
'You're okay now, lad!' I said.

—o—

28

V Day

Too late the formula for peace. Victory
Sinks to our roots like a grub in the earth,
Undiagnosed, infiltrating our life's blood,
Invisible, corrupting the green shoots.
Ugly shall be our progeny – withered in youth.
Shall they know old age
With its strange, quiet delights?
Before them lie our 'freedom' and our 'truth'…

March 1946
Takoradi, Gold Coast, W.A.

—o—

A Lullaby for World War 2

Quiet, little one,
(Soldier of twelve years hence?)
The night is wild. It seems
Darkness and hate have fearful permanence,
But hush your fears,
For time may recompense
Our bitter tears.

Sleep, dear one, sleep,
Lulled by the wind − like guns
Low rumbling, deep
In Hell, where fathers spilt life for their sons…
His fight was brief.
We are the luckier ones
Who bear the grief.

Sleep, little son.
I gave you life, through love
For one now gone…
Live to set free the dove
That is his soul,
To spread its wings across the sky above
And make men whole.

Stop asking why –
He would just fall asleep.
His lullaby
The desolate hiss of rain. He would not weep
Nor cry like you…
Oh hush, hush, child, and sleep
This nightmare through.

Year of Rearmament , 1951

—o—

Remembrance Day

Poppies are red at the Cenotaph. Wreaths
Have been laid on the parish memorial,
After the silence, the ex-soldier breathes
His relit cigarette, and the conspiratorial
Whisper of mourners awakes into voices
That talk no more now of the dead, but of dinner.
The ex-soldier thinks of his job, and rejoices –
Unemployment is less through the ranks being thinner.

So after the hell of war
The nation is impious, selfish, and scarcely remembers
For two minutes together, nor
Gives it a thought in between the Novembers.

(The civilian was thankful, left out of the strife
And the soldier was glad he came back with his life.)

But must we remember the dead only, in our grieving?
They ask us to honour the dead. All honour to them!
But I would lay my wreath (their scorn forgiving)
On the stone of those still alive; my head
Uncovered, out of deepest respect and compassion for them:
Their dying takes longer, and is miscalled living.

The civilian is not thankful: his shame
Thwarts his ambition. If the soldier spilled
His thoughts, there would be left the blame
Of conscience, for the fellow-men he killed.

Bereft or not, the minds of those alive
Are living tombs. Did anyone survive?

1951

—o—

Autumn 1950

Walking the dead fields after harvesting
The stubble pricks our shins, and crackling, lifts
Bird flocks, that, tossed upon the breeze,
Settle again. The smell of burning drifts
From damp back-garden fires, and foraging
Blackbirds rustle dead leaves beneath bare trees.

Low sun, grey cloud and air becoming cold,
Earth's movements stilled; but brief sporadic darts
In corners, indistinct, glimpsed here and there,
Betray life's rearguard, and from unseen parts
Her sounds are thin and sibilant, dry and old,
Last distant whispers of the songs that were.

So we must walk with weary, toilsome tread –
The sons of victory, among earth's stubble fields,
Recalling without joy our harvest hymn
When we admired the power our reaper wields
Over the fruits of life and toil, now dead
And lost to us. Winter approaches, grim.

With hearts and limbs benumbed by life's decay
That through the air we breathe invades our blood,
Shall we succumb again to the old lies
Of promised Spring to come – a glorious flood
Of plenty? Or can we find a way
To harvest for ourselves a new authentic prize?

—o—

Korea, 1950

They hardly knew why they should want to live
Until a promise came
From foreign parts, to strengthen them and give
Those suffering a name,
Their labouring an aim.
And then, inspired, incredulous myriads raised
A desperate, longing cry:
Through hunger, fire and steel, their lives hope-crazed,
To vindicate, or die.
When suddenly –

O what has happened? Staring
At torn corpses, in frenzy weeping,
Mother of Korea, despairing –
These are your children, sleeping!
You cannot stop screaming, lonely
Girl, scorched in your naked yearning:
Nor past nor present only,
Hope's future too, is burning.
While bomber crews returning

Report a dull operation
Upon the bodies of children, the heart of a mother, the life of a
nation.
And the tanks do not notice the slither of their tracks
Over the little bodies, through their lives' rubble churning.
What guilt might levy tax?
Christ's words? Since not in orders, not worth learning.
(Then a moment's amusement, for relief: the driver smiled
To see a savage woman prancing wild....)

Is life made happy for a moment in its course
Deeper to rend the heart?
Or love and fellowship bequeathed to us, the worse
To torture us, torn apart?
Resigned, doomed....never such agony
Blazed in their empty past,
As now, when souls and minds and bodies lie
Groping for death at last.

—o—

The Rebels

1

Pacifist

You who read beauty in a senseless world,
Proclaiming as beauty all your invented trash,
Within whose sentient mind there is no true feeling –
You have made a chariot with your own two hands
Which you are riding by perverted choice headlong to hell.

I will not join you in your chosen ride.
I will not follow to cheer at the roar of your wheels,
Nor will your scythe blades cut me down as you lose control of them.
I have my own way, and I climb a sunny hill.

I have clothes on my back, and the means of life beside me,
I have the beauty of earth and life in my heart,
While over there is the battered flesh paving your pathway
behind me,
And I will see its red blood as your emblem and go on my way.

2

A Dying Partisan

How can I be fit to speak
Before the councils of the meek?
By force I met the force of wrong
And gloried in its slain with song!

Who never turned the other cheek,
How can I be fit to speak,
That never did the sword abhor
But gloried in the clash of war?

O people that on earth do dwell
I found, who feared no other hell –
And those condemning other men
To living death, I did condemn.

Presumptuous sin? Aye, I knew well
My savage soul was doomed to hell;
But this I chose, that those oppressed
(And worthier far than I) be blessed.

I die. But free, their virtues grow.
Come hell!...This they need never know.
So! Maggot death within my breast
Eat for your life with healthy zest!

1950

—o—

Aftermath

1

War and Peace

As bitter passions churn the breasts of men
As ever in a fear-fomented brain
Conceiving utmost hell were made to reign –
Yet all are not insane.

Not from the planet Mars does war arise
But from our self-deception and our lies,
Self-righteousness provoking battle-cries –
Yet all are not unwise.

Protests of 'love for all mankind' are made,
And plans for bettering its lot are laid;
Holding to hope, the peoples ply their trade –
Yet they are all afraid.

2

Sonnet, free style

It is so little, all we know
With our best will and all our mind and heart.
How deep into the truth can understanding go?
Only the smallest part.
We see so little with our eyes and brain;
We do not feel our fellow being's woe;
Yet we would judge the measure of his pain
And how he bears its smart.
Enthrone him; crucify him… Be it so –
But we shall look into his eyes again…
And we, who would in arrogance impart
'Wisdom' and 'justice' shall ourselves, brought low,
Stand before judgment, and the journey start
Through humble selflessness true peace to gain.

1950

—o—

Danger Money

'A shilling extra a shift, lad'
The under-manager said,
'We pay them danger-money.'
    (The wages of the dead.)

'A shilling extra a shift, lad.
He knew there was gas in there.'
    (But he lay as dead as ever
    Not six yards from the air.)

'A shilling extra a shift, lad;
And he was warned as well.'
    (But they sent him in, and paid him
    A single fare to hell.)

'A shilling extra a shift, lad
Is for the risk he took.'
    (I trust the sum's recorded
    In Gabriel's audit book.)

'A shilling extra a shift, lad –
Could happen to anyone…'
    (Let's leave it as a gift, then
    To his widow and his son).

For a young miner, whose father
Was killed in a Lanarkshire pit.

42

—o—

Winterreise

Your first song ended with the words 'good-night'
And all the others had the same refrain.
Perhaps what old Catullus said was right:
We meet only to say good-bye again…
We cannot let it matter, if the ache
Must throb forever, ceaseless till we die;
Rather we must forbid the dawn to break
And stop the sun from shining in the sky!
Safe then, we'd journey in eternal night;
Then we'd meet no-one who might know or care;
Obsessed by nightmares and beset with fright –
These are the dreams that we'd find everywhere!
So the long journey leads us back to pain…
 How we would long to see the day again!

Winterreise – Song cycle by Schubert

Atque in perpetuum frater, ave atque vale

Catullus

—o—
43

Blank Verse
For one in trouble

So you have succeeded in side-tracking your attention.
By-passing your heart, you cannot feel your hurt any more.
But how sensitive you have become to the hurts of others!
How your empty heart resonates – resounding like a vault
With the echoes of other voices!
How the echoes linger, and throw back the vibrant sounds
Of all the poetry and song ever written or sung.
How unbearably, like Eugénie de Guérin,
You have the pain in your brother's breast
Even while assuring yourself it is not your own!
(After all, they are only echoes: it is only a song
Or a poem – nothing real – that rends you.)
Somebody else's thoughts too deep for tears
Have shone out from your eyes often –
Too deep for tears, or words, or any other folly,
Yet shrieking wordlessly in the way you looked, before you laughed
'Romantic stuff, Wordsworth. Waste of time, of course!'
But furtively the look still smouldered. And I watched it,
And heard the echoes too, insistently recurring,
Stifled, desperate cries for help behind the laughing, drowning.

> 'J'ai mal à la poitrine de mon frère'
> (Eugénie de Guérin)

1950

—o—

44

Separation
*Air mo thuras**

Wherever you wander, lonely child
By the silent sea, or torrents wild,
In roaring storm or in summer mild,
This I do know:
That though by mocking fate beguiled,
There I would go.

And though the years may slowly trace
The path to my last resting place,
I shall not hesitate to face
The toll of care:
For with that old familiar grace
You will be there.

*On my journey

An Islesman's longing

—o—

45

Fragments

1

Longing

Here is the only life there ever was.
This, and no other.
Rare now the fantasies we used to seek and pause
To ponder over,
Stirring like memories of an ancient book
Of dreary tales scratched by an unskilled pen,
Leaving us sad, uneasy, loath to look
Back to the futile pages once again…

Rare are they now, and rarer still becoming,
Random nostalgic smells
Of summer gardens, where the bees are humming
And calmness dwells,
Prompting sad aching for an unknown bliss
In some peaceful nirvana.
                              But can we yearn
For never-known delight?—or ever miss
The unsung songs our lips did never learn?

2

Loss

Did I once live in time, with hope and care?
Perpetual timelessness engulfs me here
And sets me in hard stone: No going on
No purpose, and no getting anywhere –
Only the screaming Now, with no time sphere
To live, or move, or be in. All is gone –
No movement from one second to the next. No fear,
No hope, no wishing. Nothingness. No night, no dawn.

1960

3

Winter

What passes for words now
(This muttering in the dark)
Spells nothing, tells nothing
Trying not to be heard.

Here is a fear that kills,
Sucking empty the heart,
Numbing the brain,
Disarticulating the voice.

This is not the pain
That stabs with a real hurt
That maddened me once,
And burst into authentic words.

Real words do not come.
Silent in its deserted house
My heart crouches, shivering.
Outside is the cold, waiting.

1992

4

Snow Buntings on the Black Hill

The year, old friend through seasons good and bad,
Is dying. Heather stumps, grey-black after the burning
Cover the hill. The air is still and sad,
All around is quiet, cloaked in a pall of mourning.
Then suddenly I see them! Flashing white wings,
Dashing among the seeds of dead grass and heather – set
So keenly on winning life out of dying things…
Small souls of hope unlooked for – so well met!

Pentlands, 1994

5

Sheep

Sheep, you are stoical in bitter weather.
You bear it simply because it is there.
You do not imagine that things ought to be better:
You do not think 'This is not fair.'

Sheep, your attitude must be commended.
Life often feels too hard to bear,
But we resent it, struggling against it
As if, somehow, hardship should not be there.

In a self-centred bubble
We double our trouble.

You use your strength to resist the storm that meets you,
Not in railing against Fate, while the storm beats you.

Pentlands, 1996

6

The Mountain

Half-way up, and into the snow.
As usual, the top seems nearer,
And the valley much farther
Than they really are.
What do I ever know
Of near or far?
As usual, illusion is clearer
Than facts are.
I struggle with my space and time.
The moment is dense as space.
I sink into it, like boots into snow
That yields as if bottomless, then gives
Just enough purchase for another pace
Into the next moment. And as I go
The mountain lives
Serenely in its own space and time.
It cannot know
The struggle in mine.

Jan. 1996

—o—

Advice

My boy, take heed: look long and well
Upon the Blessed Damozel;
Keep strength and zeal and courage for
The Universal Conqueror.
For she will lie in wait for you
And your resolve, however true,
Will tear in two.
No abstract values will survive;
In vain morality will strive
To keep poor virtue's corpse alive;
While wisdom's few
Remaining pillars fall, as fell
Good sense before.
And neither pride nor prestige nor
The self-esteem that was your shell
Shall spring up at your bidding, or
Exist at all beneath her spell.
She is your future's ancestor.
Do not deprive
Yourself of life. Look long and well.
Live if you must. But if you do,
Prepare for hell…

A joke!
1951

—o—

52

Insomnia

…The shadow forms solidify
And viscid darkness slowly seals
The cranial tomb. The tears are dry,
Thought's dizzy dancers petrify,
The spring of life congeals.
And in black cul-de-sacs the future looms –
Eternal spectre of the catacombs.

Here is the horror consciousness denies
As life drifts through the interim of days:
Days spent in following the luring cries
That from the sepulchre of childhood rise
To skip truth's toilsome maze,
And mock, as blinded reason hopes to find
The hidden purpose of confused mankind.

Now locked within my skull are hopes grown old.
I cannot sleep, nor longer try to save
Their barren leanness from the hungry cold
That grows within the bone as clammy mould
Through these safe walls that must become my grave –
As down the past for many such, whose pride
Fed on the carrion of their kind and died.

An atavistic dynasty too blind to reign,
Many outlived their end, and echo on,
Accepted by long habit, that would fain
Plead helplessness, and in time's arms remain
Asleep in ignorance, until the dawn
Of happiness (– or death? O dear God! Stay
This last irrevocable second on its way.)

I start with terror cold upon my brow
And in my thudding heart time's deadly beat:
Gone are the echoes and the dead dreams now,
As leaves, at long last severed from the bough,
Whirl and are lost along the hurrying street.
Now aimless, all believing I disown,
And face the void of nothingness alone.

But perhaps the echoes have misled me?
Strange, how in eternal hours of dread we
Try to limit them by doubt –
(Maybe nothing at all to worry about!)
Perhaps the echoes in the hollow wall
Of skull, reverberating, touched a faulty chord,
Some misconstrued remark, or some chance word
Tuned the brain out of key, and that was all.

Distorted shadows on the nursery wall
By dying firelight follow through the years.
The ageing children, overtired with play,
Who when they put their grown-up toys away
Weary for sleep, with long-forgotten fears...
Here come the tears –
Hot overflow of day's unrighted wrongs.

Flushed on the pillow of elusive peace
Cheeks unkissed spill
The bitter burden of life's loneliness
That haunts us still.
On what to cry but sleep? And now the throngs
Of hinting shadows sign to one another,
Conspiring each with each, imparting dumb
Fear-laden echoes of a cry for mother
Unheard, unanswered. Sleep will never come.

Incessantly the ticking clock
Insists on tunnelling into time,
Like hammer-blows invading rock
In narrow channels, whither flock
The ghosts of memory's pantomime.
Here echoes have a hollower tone,
Long spun in labyrinths of stone

Alone, alone, alone, alone,
Incessantly the heart-beat throbs.
Remorselessly its sullen tone
Ignores death's precipice and plods on.
My heart heeds not my sobs...
Then thought inchoate struggles clear –
It is not death, but life I fear!

My heart is marking time, my life
Is standing poised at the abyss...
Can it be I who wields the knife?
The spectral future, scorning strife
Offers more dreadful love. Its kiss
Would woo me from my thought, and vow
No more reality. Eternal now.

Struggle away? To nowhere? And my limbs
Are weak. I need some greater power, some shield
From utter loneliness...and desperation dims
The sense of horror. Drowning reason swims
In swirling floods of doubt. So, now I yield?
But reason's final cry breaks loud and long:
'Stop, suicide! A new-found thought is strong!'

Strong? With no purpose, form, direction, aim?
O do not mock me. All my dreams have gone.
They were thought's fabric, woven in a game
That was my life before awakening came,
Revealing terrible time still driving on:
I can no longer play with thoughts. And yet...
Doubt strikes again, and holds me in its net.

Perhaps there is a new life? Even here
A cloud might pass, that a new world uncovers
Uncharted ways, through which no echoes steer;
And reason, purged of dreams, help me win clear
To save not my abstracted self, but others...
If then my plight has shown that life's guide lied
Truth's yet to find, with reason as my guide.

My vision clears, the foul miasma lifts,
The blood runs warm, the spectre draws away.
Towering amorphous horror slowly drifts
Back to the nursery shadows. Now I may
See what I choose. But just before they fled
Did I an instant glimpse myself lie dead?

Why do my thoughts so surely and finally
Weave the same pattern? Always the theme
Is death: how can I argue effectively
That death is not reality, nor life mere dream?
Everything ends in death that ever lives.
It is to die again we leave the womb,
And use the torturing faculties that life gives
To stare around this antechamber of the tomb.

Incomplete. (Sometime in mid 50's)

—o—

The Cynic

You say you know what love means? So,
 let mankind kiss your feet in awe!
'Love alters not…' I hear you say,
'Tout comprendre, c'est tout pardonner.'
You may be right, if what you call
'understanding' means anything at all.

 I would take you out one early night,
or on a brilliant summer's day,
and show you what you have never sought: the sight
of the children of want and poverty at play.
Where out on the crowded streets of any town
stalks the eternal shadow. And
lonely within an ordinary room,
upon a common shabby chair,
the shadow broods. Look up and down
the length of this material land.
Observe it loom –
Blind misunderstanding everywhere.

Maybe you picked out one example, whom you saw
stand in defiance of the common law.
Perhaps you noticed in her innocent eyes
burning without hope, longing that never lies.
Perhaps you felt the challenge of her youth,
strong in revoking all our cherished 'truth.'
Perhaps you simply loved her in your way?
I do not know. It is vain anyway.

1950

—o—

58

Insanity

Our wills are still too weak,
Though little strength be needed,
how many times must the voice of reason speak
till it is heeded?
Have we assumed it is not worth our while
for harder ways to leave the infantile?

Our social obligations never found
a welcome till our fellow-men were dead:
Hands never used to till our brother's ground
have dug his grave instead.
Wishes that seek ecstatic bliss above,
frustrated, wreck the lives of those we love...
And so on. Till with self-disgust we find
that life has no sense in it –
Poor things! We are the victims of a blind
impulse of the minute.
No purpose, obviously – except to reconcile
this with our will to live in such a style.

'We're set! He's threatened suicide! Come, let's dine.'
'What?.. But…'
'Oh yes, I forgot… Ethics, of course. (Hell!
What a system!) Oh, we might as well
serve up the usual line –
Tell them our motives are just what they're not,
as if they didn't know! OK. That's fine:
A nice load of virtue we'll try to sell.
Now forget it. To business! I'll tell you what's what.'

(Swine or not, he'll win. He never failed:
Conscience and self are spliced.
Another blow is hammered at the nailed
extremities of Christ.)
And God forgives him like a child
who knows no better. There is only one
way to emend him: through the mild
glance of compassion from the suffering Son.
Jesus knew
Well enough what Judas planned to do.
The Roman soldiers merely did their job,
like GI's in Korea. Orders were orders.
And Pilate, fearing the rebellious Jewish mob,
acted to keep the peace within his borders.
The Prince of Peace is taken by a pawn
whose move's dictated by the Pentagon.

Is this serious? Ask that business man
(who's also a politician,
respectable, well-dressed and clean)
What does it mean?
He will tell you
as much as he wants you to think he knows.
And faith in his wonderful life is not a pose
he tries to sell you.
Far from it: He and God have made the world
so good to live in (he has just dined well.)
Those disagreeing ('communists') will be hurled
by him and God down into death and hell.
It's all so simple. Money is the clue
to ethics, values, creeds. It must be true.

If not, he vanishes, and all his kind.
His system perishes. His world would end
with a forced laugh – out of its mind:
Bewildered, as a schizophrenic youth,
quite seriously attempting to defend
his inner certainty of what is truth,
raises a knife, and murders his best friend.

1950

—o—

Early Spring, Langdale

I'm sick of talk when my heart is aching
Deeper than words can reach,
And tired of tears that cannot empty longing –
They are as dead as speech.

Could I have been with you as he was once:
Climbed with you, fought with you and laughed with you
again,
And wanted you into the depths of you, as he did,
What would this daily life have counted then?

Could loving you have eased the futile yearning?
No. I was not he, not he;
Yet here, shrouded closely by clinging phantoms,
Scarcely can I be me.

For I too have my passionate ghostly Other,
My own Chapel Stile to revisit in my pain.
That door too is locked, and the pale ghost cannot answer,
Yet still it draws me back through time again.

And I too batter the dark wood, and stare desperately at the
green slate walls of my own haunted places, empty and long
since dead. And in sudden fright
I am crying with my whole body and soul 'Come back! Why
did you leave me?
With terrible bitter anguish, into the night.

Lake District, 1980

—o—

62

Anger

You want all of me; and it is true
That were we equals I might want all of you.
But how much is left for either? For we start
By not being equals. I become just a part
Of your life for a minute –
Not what you really need – and in it
Flickers this soul-haunting ghost, never more than a promise…
Is this me being me?
Maybe all that I can ever hope to be.
In life, nature, music, art, there is no rest.
I try to seize beauty, but it falls apart
Into the meaninglessness of this and that.
And always a savage beast howls in my breast,
A wild dog that has its teeth in my heart
And tugs and snarls and shakes it like a rat.

1980

—o—

Enigma

Why am I grieving? Look inwards and I find
Mourning for some old death – I don't know whose.
Why are beauty and sorrow so welded in my mind?
Before you, I was dead: the silent blood
Stirred by nought warmer than archaean ooze
In some Silurian sea's primaeval slime.
Now getting closer, tears of some sad loss flood;
And I am borne through huge distances of time
Alone, adrift, on a sweet bitter sea –
In gentle waters drowning. So does love take me.

1980

—o—

Thoughts upon a poem by Yeats

'*The Coming of Wisdom with Time*'

'*Though leaves are many, the root is one;*
Through all the lying days of my youth
I swayed my leaves and flowers in the sun;
Now I may wither into the truth.'
                    WB Yeats
                    from 'The Green Helmet
                    and Other Poems' 1910.

'Though leaves are many, the root is one'
 And the root remains one, deepening with time;
 And stronger sap defies autumn's fickle sun,
 Though leaves and flowers are shed in winter's rime.

 What's true to age is naught to passing youth
 Much as it knows that withering looms ahead,
 And thinks its doomed vanity the death of truth:
 But life remains when the lying leaves are dead.

 And fairer truth than flowers of youth can know
 Arises from the withering of their pride:
 Eternal truth, whatever winds may blow
 Feeds on the false illusions that have died.

                              1980

—o—

Corsica

1

Arrival

Was this myself awakening? This a different world?
To all appearances, just another south French town…
But nothing to do with appearances, there lay curled
A strange wild creature in me, still asleep –
And everything had changed since I lay down.
I knew that from then on my company he'd keep,
To share identity. So now there was me, as seen
By my companions, and me as myself alone,
But here was this Other also, that had never been
A part of me – alive, and yet unknown,
Here in my soul's substance… Did he creep
In from the streets of Ajaccio, having flown
From some strange source that claimed me as its own?

2

Forêt de l'Ospedale

Corsica's old sweet-smelling fastnesses
Turn back so easily from well-tended coasts
To natural wilderness, changeless through centuries,
Still haunted now by old invaders' ghosts.

What troops sail out now from port in Genoa?
Can it be true that they are here no more?
Are these men dead whom I feel here around me,
Haunting the mountain maquis and the shore?

3

The Tower, Porto

I feel uneasy, sensing danger: a sudden pang of warning…
Yet the evening, calm and beautiful, has given no sign;
Someone, somewhere, is watching, as the sun is setting;
But nothing moves. No presence here but mine.

Who is waiting? Who makes no sound, no motion?
I watch the sun drop behind Cenino, and the red pool slowly fills –
A Genoese soldier watched that sunset spread like blood on the
        ocean,
Thinking of tomorrow in the hostile hills.

4

'Civitas Calvi, Semper Fidelis'

(*engraved on the Citadelle*)

Anxiety gnawed at him, painful as his hunger.
The families were starving, the food they stocked
Long gone. His brother dead… He stared around in anger:
The land was ravaged, and the sea-ways blocked.

The peasant skirted the cliffs. They had implored him
To avoid the port of Calvi. He looked down.
The French were everywhere, but he had nothing. They
ignored him.
A pall of smoke hung low above the town.

Corsica had fallen, except that heap of stones,
Heart of the Genoese, the Calvi Citadelle.
There they had fought and starved; and their dried bones
Blew with smoke in the wind. They lived in hell.

It had gone on endlessly. The man heard tell
That wives and children fought on the ramparts too;
But it was not his fight. *His* children starved as well.
The whole world burned and rotted…What to do?

He went his way home as the sun was sinking.
A Genoese patrol passed him. One turned round,
Snarled 'Sampiero's bastard!' And unthinking,
Slashed the Corsican peasant to the ground.

'Idiot! He's not a partisan' said another,
'He comes from Galeria way. I knew him well.
'Not long ago the Frenchies killed his brother.'
Said the first, 'They're all alike – so what the hell…'

They passed and left him. Calvi went on burning.
And stood as if the end would never come.
They did not yield. The French kept on returning.
The wounded peasant never made it home.

That was in 1555.
The same thing happened 200 years later, when the Citadelle was
      besieged by Paoli and the English. It was there that Nelson
      lost the sight of his right eye.
The Corsican peasant, struggling to survive, still wondered what all
      this had to do with him.
In yet another 200 years or so, in 1980, under French rule, he was
      still saying 'Intantu paghemu!' – 'Meanwhile we are
      paying…' (in a nationalist newspaper.)

1980

—o—

Japanese Style

Haiku (5-7-5)

Twittering swallows
Fuss and shiver in the air.
Below, the lake sleeps.

A trackless jungle
Incomprehensible love –
O soul, where is God?

I rescued you, tossed
From the wreck, but could not find
My Self that was lost.

Day after long day
That incredible mountain
Shone in my heart's joy.

I had so aspired
To meet you on the mountain
But perhaps you tired.

The winter's night blinds
With the darkness of parting
Eyes that cannot weep.

The small spring flower
Shrinks from the pain of sunlight
Burning on cold snow.

January rain.
Dismal are the thoughts that fall
In my mind's wet streets.

January snow.
My thoughts blowing with the wind
Whence? Where do they go?

Deep as the forest
With its unnumbered creatures
Is my heart's darkness.

So brief are their days
Blue skies and cherry blossom
And happy faces.

One lovely spring day
He died here, in lilac time.
A sweet scent lingers.

Strongly, eagerly
The crocus-shoots of desire
Pierce the lying snow.

Tanka (5-7-5-7-7)

Try and try again
In spite of all the failures
Is the message of
Evolution and of Christ.
Hear it, with both brain and heart.

Linked Verse

Thankfully I wake
Bathed in the gold of sunrise.
A new day begins.
The stormy night past,
Expectantly I long for
The calm dawn's embrace.
Wonderful indeed
To be enwrapped in sunrise
Out of the dark cold.
Seeing me tremble
There is no way Dawn could wish
To withhold her love.
Quietly she loosens
The mist's white veil from her breast
And nourishes my soul.

—o—

The Post

Here is an old postcard, a long-forgotten one,
That brings a flash of memory into my mind's drab shadow.
There are flowers, and a pretty girl smiling in the sun –
And the colours seem to brighten, as I see a summer meadow.

All peace and beauty. But this remembering opens up a door
To the recollection of an incident in war.

We had emerged from the jungle into the battlefield.
The enemy had fled, and the place was cleared
Apart from two wrecked vehicles, some smashed steel helmets,
Clips of ammunition, spent shells and other trash.
And amongst this, I saw the post-card. Suddenly, in that mess,
Here was this picture of tranquil life. I picked it up.
I felt its value. I stowed it safely. It spelled normality.
A boy and girl glad to meet in a sunlit meadow
Reminded me that such a thing existed in the world.

It had reminded its owner in his hell too, I hoped.
The meadow, flowers and people were Japanese.
The message for him was peace, sent from his distant home,
And whether he had survived, or been dragged off dead,
He had left that memory for me (the enemy) instead.

A memory of Burma, 1944

—o—

73

A Cycle of Sonnets

1

Duplicity   (P.D.K)

Complacent, fearless, see the self-made heads:
Behold the timid, cringing Self withdrawn –
Insatiable and satisfied in one,
The many-headed Lernian Hydra treads.
In the green Meadows oft his form he spreads
To trap the she-goat prey he feeds upon;
His soul-shape gilding sundown and the dawn
The stronger pities and the weaker dreads.
O fabled beast! After a heavy meal
The stomach hates the very sight of food,
Yet, having many heads, you can reveal
That in this evil there may yet be good,
For though some heads a little sick may feel,
A morsel choice may suit Some Other's mood.

2

Rationality   (J.P.D)

Born for Olympus in this puny world is he,
A Giant, tied with Lilliputian chains,
A mighty charger straining at the reins,
A captive lion, fighting to be free.
In his present, things that are to be
Exist, but yet this being still remains
Unrealised, because despite his pains
No greatness can man fashion from vacuity;
And with the minute tools of such a land
As our poor earth, and with its useless stone,
The reason-guided, intellect-driven hand
Cannot create a palace out of sand,
And foreign in our land remains Alone,
Dreaming of Majesty, on far Perfection's strand.

3

Inferiority (R.C.M)

In some ways he may not have more than most
(I speak of him, but O how like to me!)
Because of this, he takes himself to be
In some ways less in All things than the host.
Dissatisfaction, hunger for the lost,
Deep sighing for some sweet Eternity
Is how he greets the world, for it to see
How roughly on the storms of life he's toss'd.
For winning what the Maker has not given
Is a hard task, and must be done alone:
And after you have laboured long, and striven,
Pleasures are few, and gains there may be none;
While in Inertia is some kind of Heaven,
And Pleasure gained from Pity's easily won.

4

Purity   (H.J.M.A)

Brilliant with sparkling sunshine, snowy-white,
Immaculate, unsullied stands the stone
Which like Debussy's pure, clear-crystal tone.
Shines freshly in the mind's soul-searching light.
Hard with unyielding force in its own right,
No Reason had the Marble of its own
Till with relentless hand the Guiding One
To his own will carved deeply wrong and right,
These features are the character we see,
The attitude unquestioning, serene,
Pressed by another, received trustingly–
Another's moral ethic which has been
The conduct-standard of humanity
For this young Living Statue of a Queen.

5

Frivolity   (R.M.P. & Co.)

'Let us inter our sorrow in the past,
'Giving it gay abandon for a shroud,
'While burying-songs of laughter singing loud
'With nails of Wit we fix the coffin fast'.
Only in ignorance can we make joy last
O singer of the song: then seek the crowd
Of frivolous pleasure-lovers who have vowed
Allegiance to Lethe's soul, and with them cast
All trouble in her water. For 'tis joy
That drives the universe along, and Pleasure –
The strongest force that Nature can employ
To gain her ends – gives in the fullest measure
The best in Life that nothing can destroy –
A blind, and wisdom-free, and priceless treasure.

6

Thoughtlessness   (B.H.)

For some short spell I knew that love was sweet
And wondrous worlds I fathomed in her eyes;
She taught me where Earth's fairest beauty lies,
And led me laughing, swift on elfin feet
(Herself a child in ignorance) to greet
Truth in his glory, shining from the skies.
Then in that searching light that never dies
Her eyes shone emptily, and would not meet
My own. Alas! How lightly flew her Soul
From the frame I knew! And heedlessly
It leads another heart towards the goal
Of happiness and love. And now to me
Her eyes are strange, and distant as the Pole:
No light of Thought or Feeling can I see.

For some fellow-students, 1938

—o—

79

Arakan

This area lies in western Burma, running south from the Indian border. It has several hill ranges from which many streams originate and track through jungle, forming rivers that flow into the Bay of Bengal. The vegetation in the hill tracts is dense mixed jungle in the south with trees and dense undergrowth, giving way to thick bamboo jungle further north. Weather conditions during the S.W. monsoon are easy to imagine – torrential rains that make the passage of troops in any numbers virtually impossible. The rivers are hugely flooded and swampy. The incidence of malaria at these times is high. Tracks are flooded, and trade is brought to a standstill. The whole district is 'dead' except for launch traffic in some areas. Our fight against malaria was vital, otherwise casualties from disease would have been more than those from contact with the enemy. Dysentery and sand-fly fever in drier times were very prevalent, while in the rivers and swamps leeches were common. These parasites could easily get through the lace-holes of boots. Two pairs of socks were helpful! To quote from the official manual: 'If a leech does take a grip on you, *do not pull it off.* The jaws will remain behind and fester, or the mouth will remain behind and continue to suck. Instead, apply a lighted cigarette, smouldering match, salt or a little lime juice... The puncture may continue to bleed for a time, because the leech injects an anticlotting fluid...' Other parasites include ticks, which are capable of carrying disease. These had to be scraped off, not pulled. Insects of all shapes and sizes abound, and snakes inhabit the undergrowth and marshes, but I never saw a case of snake-bite. At night there were constant sounds of animal life, from loud high-pitched screaming to sinister growls. And of course one had to be alert for any sound of enemy patrols.

I have added this gratuitous appendage to this little book as a background to what were writings about the periphery of war, made during periods in hospital, on leave, and after demobilisation. As a Medical Officer my unrelenting battle was against disease.

Also from Augur Press

On a Dog Lead by Mirabelle Maslin
ISBN 978-0-9549551-5-1   £6.99

This is a collection of essays, short stories and reflections to aid any reader who wants to look more deeply at what is happening in daily life. The author is a therapist of many years' experience.

In our society, we are mostly helped to see what we are meant to see. But each household has much that is hidden from view, and society itself shares many tacitly-agreed 'blindnesses'. Those who comment openly upon these find that they have a mixed reception. The Tale of the Emperor's New Clothes is far from having lost its relevance.

We are likely to continue to enact the habits and belief systems which we have absorbed since birth unless we make attempts to examine this whole area in an objective light. The process of becoming aware is a positive one, although it can often provoke feelings of shock and denial.

Order from your local bookshop, amazon or from the Augur Press website www.augurpress.com

Beyond the Veil by Mirabelle Maslin
ISBN 0-9549551-4-5 £8.99

Spiral patterns, a strange tape of music from Russia, a 'blank' book and an oddly-carved walking stick...

Ellen encounters Adam, a young widower, and a chain of mysterious and unpredictable events begins to weave their lives together. Chance, contingency and coincidence all play a part – involving them with friends in profound experiences, and lifting the pall of loss that has been affecting both their lives.

Against a backdrop of music, plant lore, mysterious writing and archaeology, the author touches on deeper issues of bereavement, friendship, illness and the impact of objects from the past on our lives. Altered states, heightened sensitivities and unseen communications are explored, as is the importance of caring and mutual understanding.

The story culminates in an experience of spiritual ecstasy, leading separate paths to an unusual and satisfying convergence.

Order from your local bookshop, amazon or from the
Augur Press website www.augurpress.com

Augur Press

For a full list of titles visit Augur Press at:

www.augurpress.com

Lightning Source UK Ltd.
Milton Keynes UK
UKOW030059270812

198135UK00001B/2/P